PULBROOK & GOULD'S

Flowers for Special Occasions

PULBROOK & GOULD'S

Flowers for Special Occasions

Photography by David Levin

B T Batsford Ltd London

We wish to dedicate this book to all staff – past and present – who have played a great part in the creation of Pulbrook & Gould.

Acknowledgement

The photographs on pages 82, 84, 85, and 86, are reproduced by courtesy of *Homes and Gardens*.

First published 1982
Reprinted 1984
© Pulbrook and Gould Ltd 1982

ISBN 0 7134 4473 8

Printed in Hong Kong
for the publisher B T Batsford Ltd
4 Fitzhardinge Street, London W1H 0AH

Contents

Introduction

The worldwide appreciation of flowers is ever increasing, and the art of flower arranging, the natural evolution of this interest, is becoming more and more popular. Styles and methods vary considerably from country to country, according to climate, prevailing tastes and the availability of materials. But whatever form the arrangements take there is little doubt that the more flowers become part of one's life the more they are loved for themselves, rather than for the manner in which they may be displayed.

Freedom of personal expression, in flower arranging as in any art form, is often the key to success. We have always believed that individuality, rather than strict rules, should be allowed to determine the style of arrangement. Such a philosophy cannot be applied to the lovely Japanese arrangements, for which the techniques are rigidly controlled, but it does underlie the free-flowing style on which our reputation has been built.

Accepted principles of design and balance, and an understanding of the many ways in which colours and textures may be used and blended to fit in with their surroundings are all helpful but they should be regarded as guidelines only, to be adapted and varied freely according to personal taste. Although studied set pieces, which conform strictly to rules of proportion and shape, give pleasure to many people, we believe that equal pleasure can be derived from our more flexible approach.

One of the first things to consider is the purpose for which flowers are going to be arranged. They may be required simply for informal day-to-day decoration in your home, or for special events, such as weddings or parties when more impact or grandeur is called for, or for occasions with a particular atmosphere, such as a barbecue or a Christmas party. The number of people to be present should also have a bearing on the choice of flowers and their arrangement. In a crowded room, for instance, small intimate bowls, however lovely, will have little effect, whereas one dramatic arrangement, clearly visible over people's heads, will make an impact straightaway, emphasising the fact that it is a special occasion.

Another thing to take into account is the style and colour of the background, so that the flowers blend with their setting. Generally speaking, if this is simple and uncluttered an elaborate display of mixed flowers will be seen to great advantage, as will an arrangement of branches and foliage with pronounced lines or sculptured shapes. If the setting is more complicated, as with many modern wallpapers, a simple mass of flowers in one of the colours in the background will be most dramatic.

The blending and contrasting of colours in an arrangement is essentially a matter of personal taste, but it is valuable to have an understanding of how the best results are likely to be achieved. In the countryside one can see how different flowers and foliage complement each other. There are two basic groups of colours: the bright ones, which are often called advancing colours and which have immediate impact, and the softer ones, which have a more subtle influence and are called receding ones.

The choice of colours will depend not only on those present in the background, but also on the light available. For instance, when flowers are going to be placed against a dark background or in a dimly lit position, one's choice is automatically restricted to advancing colours. The muted tones of blue, mauve and green will be largely unnoticed, whereas colours such as red, orange, yellow and white will show up well and even gain in importance.

If an arrangement is lit chiefly from one side by a slanting light it is a good plan to have most of the darker shades on the well-lit side and vice versa. To avoid cutting the arrangement into two halves, however, some of the paler shades must be spread over the whole arrangement.

In artificial light the majority of flowers look best when lit from above. When lit from behind very little will show up, apart from the outline of the arrangement and any exposed stems.

The different shapes and habits of flowers and foliage can be used in endless combinations to provide interest and variety. A 'fussy' flower with a background of sculptured leaves can look quite different from its appearance with a more delicate foliage, and the same applies to a flower of simple form against different foliage backgrounds.

A few other observations on the subject of colour are worth making here. Pale yellow flowers, when added to a basically pink arrangement, give a moonlight quality and look enchanting. The hard yellows, however, are less versatile and are best used within their own colour range. We believe that clashing colours, from orange to red, pink and even mauve, can look splendid together, but no rules can be laid down for mixing these colours; the real artist will avoid the dangers inherent in such bold combinations.

It is well worth experimenting with a wide range of textures and shapes to discover the varying, and sometimes elusive, qualities of different flowers and foliage. Their appreciation and use are especially important in some monochromatic arrangements, for example in 'all-green' and 'all-grey' displays. Much skill is required of the arranger if each piece of material is to contribute some distinctive quality. When this is achieved, an all-foliage group can be quite as beautiful and dramatic as one that includes the most exotic flowers. In order to get the best effect from each flower, leaf or spray, their natural lines and shapes must be preserved and not distorted. When you are picking them bear in mind the way they are to be used. Usually you will prefer curving pieces to straight ones, with some bending to the right, some to the left and some forwards, to suit various positions in your arrangements.

Be careful not to waste the leaves on the stems by

The old-fashioned quality of this arrangement in a rush basket makes it a perfect complement to an old Welsh dresser, and the flowers, love-in-a-mist (*Nigella damascena*), corn flowers (*Centaurea cyanus*), wild ox-eye daisies and grasses, continue the colouring of the plates.

removing them unnecessarily. They can be invaluable for giving body, or fullness, to an arrangement, and they will also conveniently hide any supporting material. If a stem is stripped of leaves and another type of foliage is substituted, the result will not have the same charm, unless it happens that the 'second foliage has a suitable dramatic colour or shape. Nature usually has her own way of harmonizing flowers and leaves. Any unwanted leaves can always be stripped off as the arrangement progresses, but we feel that they should only be removed entirely if this would increase the decorative or lasting values of the flower. However, all leaves that will come under the water-line ought to be stripped.

Of all the points mentioned above no single one is vitally important, but they are all guidelines which we keep constantly at the back of our minds as we go through the various stages of arranging flowers, from ordering the materials to finishing the decorations.

Care and Treatment

When picking flowers the first thing to remember is that this must be done in the cool of the evening or early morning; if they are picked in the heat, even without sunshine, they are apt to wilt. Then, the shorter the delay before they are put into water the longer they will last. The ideal method of picking, therefore, is to take a bucket of water with you round the garden, so that the stems can be put in water immediately. But how often is this practicable or even possible? Almost never.

After picking, all material should be put into deep water as soon as possible and left in a cool place for several hours. Exactly the same procedure should be applied to flowers and foliage that have been bought.

We suppose that just as many people, if not more, buy flowers from a shop as pick them from their gardens, so we felt it might be helpful to give a little advice on what to look out for, or at least what to dodge, when buying flowers. Never buy flowers that have been lying in boxes, for any length of time, in the hot sun outside a shop. If spring flowers show any sign of transparency, give them a wide berth. Flowers with a daisy formation should only be bought if their yellow centres are hard and tinged with green. Hard

stamens mean that a flower has just opened, but stamens covered with powdery loose pollen indicate that it is further advanced and will last a shorter time. Fortunately growers are now very conscious of the benefit of sending flowers to market in a backward condition. This makes it easier to buy many kinds of flowers, such as daffodils, irises, tulips, lilies and gladioli, in tight bud, so gaining not only a longer life for the flowers, but also the pleasure of watching their gradual growth into full bloom. However, it is not advisable to do this in every case. Roses, if bought in very tight bud, may not always open in water. It is best to buy these when some colour is showing. When picking flowers in the garden the same points should be borne in mind.

Flowers bought from a shop will obviously have to be out of water for some time. Even when the journey home is short, the stems should have their ends snipped off and be put into water as soon as convenient, for a long deep drink before they are arranged. A good florist will have given the stems the best treatment, usually just a diagonal cut, but special treatment is required for some types of stem, so a few guidelines will be given below.

Whether they have come from a florist or straight from a garden, all flowers should be handled as little as possible. A basket or box in which to carry the flowers may be rather unwieldy, but it can save a great deal of damage.

Hard woody stems, such as those of chrysanthemums, shrubs and most trees, are more likely to survive well if the ends are hammered for about 2.5 cm (1 in) from the bottom of the stem, or slit with a sharp knife for 5-7 cm (2-3 in), the outer skin being peeled off. Take care not to be too heavy-handed with the hammer, or the stem will be rather shorter than you intended. Hollow-stemmed flowers require more specific treatment, so we will mention some of the ones we use a great deal. Dahlias and angelica benefit from having the ends of their stalks put in 5 cm (2 in) of boiling water for about ten minutes, whereas cow parsley is best plunged into cold water. Delphiniums and lupins cause us much concern because of the almost daily fall of florets, but this can be reduced to a minimum if the stems are filled with water and plugged with a small piece of wet cotton wool, until they are placed in an arrangement. However, this is so time-consuming that we find it feasible only if the stems are to be out of water for a considerable time.

With bulbous flowers the flower stem is white until it reaches the surface of the ground, and this white part should be cut off to encourage absorption of water. Tulips and bluebells are the kinds that respond best to this treatment, but all are helped.

Some kinds of stem have a tendency to bleed. Among these, euphorbias are the ones we use most frequently. Their stems contain a milky substance which can cause skin irritation and they will only last well if the ends of their stems are sealed. This can be done either by burning them, or by standing them in 5 cm (2 in) of boiling water until the bleeding stops. Burning the ends of poppy stems makes the flowers last longer.

Another group of flowers which gives us trouble is the hellebore family. The Christmas rose (*Helleborus niger*) does not present many problems; it is the varieties with several heads to a stem that can be such a nightmare. But they are so lovely, they are worth special care. They survive best if they are picked only after the seedhead has formed on the first flower. Prick them just behind the head with a sharp pin, and at intervals the entire length of the stem, and then put them in tepid water up to their heads. The pricking

treatment will also help tulips to revive quickly, but these should not be put in very deep water.

Bracken and ferns will curl far less quickly if they are laid for a while in a thin solution of starch and water.

Some flowers, like hydrangeas and violets, will last better or revive more quickly if their petals are moist. If you do not have a syringe, you can put the heads in cold water and then shake them gently to remove excess moisture.

There are some flowers which will last much longer if their foliage is removed, for example shrubs such as *Philadelphus* (commonly, though mistakenly, call 'syringa'), *Weigelia* and lilac (*Syringa*). In some cases stripping off the leaves reveals lovely flowers that are otherwise barely visible; lime, for instance, with its delicate flowers and pale green wings borne on dark brown branches, is unrivalled for midsummer arrangements if all the leaves are removed.

This practice of showing off flowers without their surrounding foliage reminds one that many flowers naturally appear before the leaves. Trees which produce exciting flowers long before the leaves appear include the wych elm, with its trusses of bright green heads, and the maples, which have clusters of lime green or apricot flowers depending on the variety. To prevent the clusters of flowers from dropping, the best method with all of these is to plunge the stems into boiling water when their ends have been hammered.

Boiling water is a wonderful aid for most wilting flowers, or for any that have been out of water for a considerable time. But it can do much damage to really soft stems, for which warm water should be quite sufficient. If you are unable to give flowers a long drink before arranging them, it is advisable, with practically every variety of stem, to use warm water.

Cutting stems under water is also a useful technique. It prevents any possibility of an air lock in the stem, and although, with the quantities we have to prepare, we are unable to do this, it is worth doing when you have only a few flowers to treat.

Having taken a great deal of trouble to pick, prepare and arrange your flowers, do remember that water is quickly absorbed when a number of stems are in the same container. A daily topping-up with water will make the flowers and foliage last longer.

Finally, there are various products on the market designed to help flowers last longer, but it is our belief that the practices we have advocated above are far more effective. This is borne out by the many remarks made on how well our flowers last, and by the small number of complaints we receive.

Vases and Containers

Anyone who becomes interested in arranging flowers and plants will develop an eye for the container most likely to show them off to the greatest advantage in any particular arrangement. A container is not just a vessel for holding water, but a most important part of the total design. It would obviously be very helpful to the flower arranger to have a large selection, but a basic range of shapes and sizes may be quite small and yet provide adequate equipment for most occasions.

Vases with a stem, such as goblets or tazzas, give a natural elegance to an arrangement, and a wine glass is ideal for a small arrangement. Bowls of all sizes are useful, and a very wide bowl is essential for a pedestal arrangement, which will have long flowing stems. For a dining-table a low container is required, so that the flowers can be kept well below eye-level. Unsophisticated flowers will look happy in pottery, especially when it is not glazed on the outside.

Silver, copper, bronze and pewter containers are lovely for arranging flowers. A container of highly polished copper or bronze, filled with the golds and reds of autumn, will bring a welcoming warmth to a dark corner of a room. More than this, metal seems to help flowers last longer.

Urns and bowls made of alabaster or marble are also good. Their colours blend perfectly with all kinds of flowers and colour combinations.

Glass, which used to be so popular, is rather out of favour these days, perhaps because of the difficulty of hiding the wire netting. If it is required, wire netting should be kept near the top of the vase and not be allowed to extend below the stems. Another reason, perhaps, is that glass so quickly becomes discoloured and stained. It needs frequent scrubbing with soap and water, and an occasional rub over with a piece of lemon dipped in salt, or rinsing with domestic bleach. Some people find that keeping a small piece of charcoal in the water will minimize this problem.

For informal arrangements with simple flowers, such as marigolds, daisies, or nasturtiums, containers made of natural materials are particularly suitable. Simple baskets made of wickerwork, raffia or rush can be very attractive. Those sold by florists usually have a liner to hold the water, but any basket can be provided with some watertight container, such as a small tin or bowl, to act as a liner, and this can be packed firmly into position with newspaper or tissue if necessary. However, now that we have flower foam it is no longer essential that a container should be watertight. It can be lined with a piece of thick polythene and then filled with a block of 'Oasis'. Either method, of course, could be used with wooden vessels too.

A low, flat dish is a great asset if you hope to do modern 'line' arrangements, or those featuring water, and a specimen vase, for the display of one lovely bloom, should be in any collection of vases and containers.

Vases are available in endless variety, and they make excellent gifts for flower-arranging friends. But the use of unconventional containers as well greatly increases one's scope. Many objects in an average home could be successfully pressed into service as flower containers. A low ovenware dish may be just right for a table decoration, or a silver sugar bowl for an all-round display; a candlestick of silver, china, brass or wood could be transformed, with the addition of a candlecup, and used for a miniature pedestal display. Candlecups come in gold, silver or black. Many other suitable candidates may have been relegated to the back of a cupboard: a tea pot, coffee pot or tureen that has lost its lid, a large cup without a handle, a china vegetable dish or sauce boat discoloured by too great a heat in the oven. All these have possibilities.

Antique markets and junk shops can provide still further and fascinating variety. You may be able to acquire a copper kettle at a reasonable price, or a preserving pan, which would be useful for containing plants, a tea urn, some lovely piece of old china, a handsomely decorated chamber pot, an old wooden tea caddy, an old-fashioned salt box such as used to hang on the wall of a kitchen. The only thing to be careful about is the danger of being 'too fancy'. With polythene and 'Oasis' available these containers need not be watertight, and chips and blemishes can easily be hidden from view with leaves and trailing stems.

Aids and Equipment

With the increase in leisure and further education, flower arranging has attracted the interest of a far greater number of people. Thus a new market has been created for a wide range of equipment and aids and these are now easily obtainable. They make it possible for the amateur to attempt and, to some degree at least, to achieve the versatility in style and design that was previously exclusive to professional florists with long years of training behind them.

The basic requirements are few: a cutting tool, some means of holding flowers in the required position, and a container. There are, however, a few other aids which every enthusiast should have:

a pair of florist's stub scissors

a pair of secateurs for cutting thick woody stems

wire netting, preferably with 5 cm (2 in) mesh

pinholders, of which there are many shapes and sizes

flower foam, which is a water-retaining substance sold under several brand names

'Oasis' fix and tape, for securing pinholders, flower foam and wire netting

a watering can with a long spout

flower tubes for making large arrangements

florist's wires, both reel wire and stub wires in several lengths and gauges

a syringe, which is most useful for keeping flowers and house plants fresh

a dustsheet, which is a great time-saver

Florist's stub scissors These are very strong, and they have a serrated edge so that stems can be cut with ease. They should also have a notch at the base of the blade for cutting stub wires. Some people prefer to use a pruning knife, but then they will need a pair of wirecutters as well.

Secateurs These are ideal for cutting thick, woody stems. It is a good idea to keep a pair in the car so that any branches you collect can be cleanly cut, without damage to trees and bushes.

Wire netting Of all flower supports, this is the most versatile and inexpensive. Galvanized wire with a 5 cm (2 in) mesh is the most suitable because it crumples easily and yet will support stems of all sizes. The amount of wire required will depend on the size and shape of the container; a bowl, of course, will require a greater quantity than a tall narrow-necked vase. If a front-facing arrangement is being done, slightly more netting will be needed at the back of the vase where the stems will be put in upright. The thickness of the stems to be used must also be considered. For an all-round arrangement the wire should be thicker in the centre of the vase. For a really large group of flowers the wire should be mounted high to give maximum support to heavy stems. In all cases the wire should be crumpled, not folded, so that the strands are in all directions.

Plastic-covered wire netting is obtainable in green

An épergne of border carnations and maidenhair fern make a colourful centrepiece for a small buffet party. Maidenhair fern will remain fresh much longer if it is floated for a while in a thin solution of starch and water.

and white. It is particularly useful if an arrangement is to be done in a precious container, and one wants to reduce the risk of this being scratched or stained by rust, but it is considerably more bulky and less pliable than uncovered wire.

All wire should be well washed after use.

Pinholders These are without doubt the most practical piece of equipment for modern or line arrangements. They should be heavy and rustless. Since they are very expensive, it is wiser to have one large pinholder, which can be used for all sizes or arrangement and all weights of stem, rather than several of different sizes. A small pinholder has a very limited use.

When the container is still quite dry, the pinholder should be firmly anchored in position by means of a small ball of 'Oasis' fix or plasticine. This is stuck to the bottom of the pinholder which is then pressed down firmly in position.

After use pinholders should always be given a good scrub, to prevent the pins from becoming clogged.

Special pinholders with only a few pins are also available. These are designed to secure 'Oasis' in a low bowl and are well worth considering.

Flower foam There are many brands of flower foam. We tend to use 'Oasis'; old habits die hard, and so it is this one that will be mentioned throughout this book, but it is worth experimenting with them all to find out which suits you best.

These water-absorbent materials have given us all the opportunity of arranging flowers in a wide variety of styles and positions far more quickly and easily than before their introduction. They also give the flowers a longer life. Beside their standard use, in a vase or bowl, they can be used to support flowers in places where it would be impossible or impracticable to have a container, such as at the top of a marquee pole, against a trellis, or in baskets that do not have a watertight lining. In the old days we had to use moss pads, and all the material had to be laboriously wired before being jabbed into the moss.

It is absolutely essential to make sure that the 'Oasis' is thoroughly soaked right through before use – an hour under water is usually long enough. It can be used for as long as it remains intact, but do remember that it should not be allowed to dry out, because it will not absorb water so well a second time. It is best to keep it moist in a plastic bag whenever it is not in use. Do not soak it for too long or it will become so spongey that the stems are only inserted with difficulty.

In low bowls we generally put a layer of wire netting over the 'Oasis' to hold it in position. Tall, solid pyramids of flowers, fruit and vegetables can be built up to any height, according to the number of blocks of 'Oasis' being used. If large displays are planned, the foundation can be kept solid by wrapping wire netting around the blocks of 'Oasis'. A small standard tree can be made with a stick, one end firmly fixed in a pot and the other bearing a small piece of 'Oasis', also firmly fixed in position, to serve as a base for the flowers.

'Oasis' fix and tape   'Oasis' fix and tape are ideal for keeping pinholders in position, and the tape can be used to hold 'Oasis' or wire netting in a container. The outside of the container must be completely dry if the tape is to have a firm grip.

A watering can with a long spout   This is essential. It enables you to fill up the container without disturbing the arrangement.

Flower tubes   When a large group of flowers is to be arranged, and there is not sufficient long-stemmed material available, one can avoid a feeling of desperation by making sure that there are some flower tubes to hand. Tubes are small, watertight, inverted cones, made of metal or plastic, which can be fixed on sticks of any length in order to give a display its required height. Tubes should be thought of as providing extra length to the stems, and not as secondary containers, or one risks giving the arrangement a very stiff, unnatural appearance.

Having chosen a stick or cane of the height you require, attach the tube to this with a stub wire, and also, perhaps, 'Oasis' tape to prevent the wire from slipping down the stick. Bamboo canes are not suitable as they tend to slip on wire netting. Always fill tubes with water as you go along. It can be hard to locate them later on, if this has been forgotten, without disturbing a finished display. It is, of course, absolutely essential to choose suitable materials to use in tubes. They must be those that might be expected to grow naturally to the height you are giving them. A delphinium, for instance, would be ideal for a top spray, whereas a marigold would look absurd and give a completely artificial effect.

Florist's wires   Reel wire, obtainable in three or four different thicknesses, is flexible, whereas stub wires are stiff and come in many different lengths and thicknesses. Both are obtainable in black or silver, and one's choice of colour depends on the background. We seldom go out on a job without a reel in our pocket and at least a small selection of stub wires in the flower box. Reel wire is useful for keeping wire netting in position. One end of a strand is secured to the netting, and then the wire is run underneath the vase and up the other side, where the other end is made firm. Another strand, secured in the same way and running at right angles to the first, will make the wire netting absolutely firm. How disheartening it would be to have an arrangement capsize when it was nearly finished. Stub wires are used for fixing tubes on to sticks, as described above, for supporting or replacing stems, and for a great variety of odd jobs.

A syringe   Although, perhaps, a syringe could be called a luxury aid, it can be extremely useful. There are occasions when flower arrangements have, of necessity, to be completed the day before they are required, and then a light spray of water will help to preserve the freshness of the blooms, as well as giving them a delightful appearance. A syringe is also very useful in maintaining house plants.

A dustsheet   This, to us, is a must. Primarily it protects the floor or carpet from leaves and bits of stalk, but it also enables you to lay all your materials around you, so that you can see clearly what you have. If, before you begin an arrangement, you place the long-stemmed materials on one side, and those with large faces on the other, you will be able to form a clear idea in your mind as to where the different pieces will show to best advantage. Obviously it is a good thing if the dustsheet is waterproof.

Design and Technique

With so many flower arranging books on the market a great deal of advice has been given on the subject of correct proportions in an arrangement, in relation to the container. Unhappily what were intended as guidelines have frequently been interpreted as rules, with the result that self-expression and originality of thought are destroyed.

We have always been against the formality and unnatural regularity of tightly arranged compositions, and so correct proportions will not be discussed here. We believe, in any case, that these will depend on the choice of container, and the shape of the materials being used. To take some examples: a solid, heavy metal vase will give visual balance to a larger arrangement than a delicate china vase of identical size, and tall, gently arching sprays of 'syringa' can be arranged much more expansively than large-headed chrysanthemum blooms, and still look in proportion to the same vase. Both instances illustrate how unwise it would be to follow guidelines to the letter. However, we hope that the basic principles and ideas given in this section will be helpful to you.

When planning a display, remember that its size should be dictated by the occasion and the setting. First of all, select the container most suitable for the size of the arrangement and the position in which it is to be placed, and make sure that you will be able to prepare this container with the necessary aids and equipment. Then decide on the materials required to achieve the desired effect. Very broadly speaking, the various parts of an arrangement call for particular kinds of material: the flowers and branches most suitable for forming the shape and outlines of a design will probably be quite different in character from those required for the face of the arrangement, or again, perhaps, from the intermediate flowers which integrate the outline materials with the focal point.

For background materials, in spring and summer, there is a wonderful variety from which to choose: flowing branches of cherry, pear, apple and 'syringa'; foliage of all shapes and textures; delphiniums, foxgloves and hollyhocks; trailing roses and honeysuckle, and any long-stemmed flowers with a graceful habit. In autumn and winter there are the branches of deciduous trees and shrubs, their leaves turned to rich autumn colours, the curving stems carrying hips, haws and other berries and old man's beard, and the evergreens. The face of the arrangement is where the larger flowers, such as peonies, lilies, hydrangeas, roses and rhododendrons, are best displayed. To create the links between these flowers and the background, and generally to 'fill-in' the arrangement, medium-sized materials are required, such as stocks, snapdragons, and spray chrysanthemums.

It may be a help to you to be given some idea of how to achieve a proper balance, in an arrangement, between outline materials and those with a large head. The proportions vary, of course, with the design, but, very generally, a front-facing arrangement requires about equal quantities, and an all-round one should be composed of roughly one third outline material to two thirds larger-faced flowers. Obviously all this applies only to groups of mixed flowers, but groups of only one type of flower should never be thought of as less exciting. In many situations they provide the most attractive and suitable kind of decoration.

Our arrangements usually conform to one of three basic shapes: the front-facing and the all-round have been mentioned above, and the third is the pyramid. But with each one there is a broad range of interpretation. The first we use for large groups and for all arrangements placed against a wall or other background. This shape is in fact more accurately described as being without a back, since the arrangements are usually very three-dimensional and may appear quite deep when viewed from the sides.

All-round arrangements, as one would expect, are for positions where the flowers will be viewed from every angle. The principles for arranging this shape apply to any size of arrangement, to a centrepiece for a small dining table as much as to a large, central arrangement in a spacious hall.

Pyramids we do in two main forms. These share the same basic shape, but one has a solid foundation of 'Oasis' or moss, which is very suitable when fruit or vegetables are to be incorporated in the arrangement, and the other, which we call a fountain, has the flowers arranged in tiered tins which we have made for us. The number and size of the tiers determine the final dimensions of the arrangement. Wire netting or 'Oasis' is put in the tins, and when the flowers are arranged the tins are filled as if they were separate containers. By using these tiers one can achieve a more delicate outline, and a much lighter, freer effect, than would be possible with a solid base. These tiered containers can be made of zinc, but this is now so expensive that tin is used instead. Do remember that they must be painted inside and out to prevent rust.

Before starting an arrangement, always make sure that the container is three-quarters full of water. It can be filled up when the arrangement is finished. If there is too much water at the beginning there may be a disastrous overflow later on. It is not a good idea to do the arrangement 'dry' and put all the water in later: flower stems keep their position better when in water, and also, of course, they will only be out of water for the absolute minimum time. When placing the stems in position try to create the impression that they are all issuing from one invisible point. Be careful not to let them cross each other.

We start our front-facing arrangement by placing the first upright stem two-thirds of the way back in the vase. This means that there is room for some of the outline material to flow slightly backwards, so giving the arrangement a far softer appearance, especially when viewed from the sides. Some of the front flowers we place in a recessed position and others we make to protrude from the arrangement. In this way the flowers lose none of their dramatic impact, but a hard, solid mass is avoided. This is important whatever kinds of flower are used here. If the flowers

An enchanting arrangement of summer flowers adding a pool of sunshine to a very beautiful dark mahogany screen, using roses, border carnations, nigella, lilies, grasses and alchemilla.

are not so large as to form a mass, when put in at the same length, they will create a pin-cushion effect, which is also to be avoided. The next step is to fill in the gaps between the outline and the front until the arrangement is complete.

For all-round arrangements we like the tall materials, which determine the size of the display, to have soft shapes; straight hard stems can give a very spikey appearance. Again for the sake of softness, we would use two or three stems to obtain the height, rather than one placed absolutely upright in the container, which would make a hard, formal apex. It is important to have five or more stems to form the circumference; when only four stems are used it is difficult to avoid a square appearance. As in a front-facing arrangement, some of the larger-faced flowers should be recessed and others made to protrude, and they should be integrated completely with the tall flowers that have formed the shape.

Small displays for a dinner-table should be built up in the same manner, but with smaller flowers, and with delicate spikes and trails to remove any feeling of solidity. With a long table decoration you should take care over positioning the outline material, the stems which give the height and length, in order to avoid giving the impression that two flat-backed arrangements have been put together.

Pyramid arrangements, with a solid base, are composed mainly of full-faced blooms, sculptured leaves, fruit and vegetables, with a few wispy trails of foliage or sprays of berries to soften the outline. It is not necessary to have any long-stemmed materials. The foundation of these pyramids can be made with blocks of 'Oasis', and can be built up to any height, and held in position by a cane running through the centre from top to bottom. The corners and the top have been rounded off, and wire netting has been wrapped round the whole thing to prevent disintegration. A single block will be sufficient for a centrepiece to decorate a table, and for an evening party a candle could be inserted into the top, to give a festive touch.

Fountains require flowers quite opposite in type to those used in pyramids. Heavy flowers would completely obliterate the delicate design, which calls for light, arching sprays and flowers with a soft flowing movement.

Apart from these three main categories of arrangement, each characterized by a basic shape, there are two others which should also be mentioned: massed arrangements and modern arrangements.

Some flowers, like marigolds, polyanthus and floribunda roses, are particularly suitable for massed displays. These are quick to do and they can be most decorative. All stems are cut to approximately the same length, and the flowers are then arranged with their heads just above the rim of the container, to form a pool of colour. Even daffodils can be arranged in this fashion; they acquire a totally new look and an unexpected beauty. Floribunda roses are ideal because when they are massed in deep water on short stems, their life span is considerably longer than when they are left on a long stem. In an arrangement of this kind it is colour, rather than shape and texture, that attracts attention. A similar massed effect can be obtained using a shallow container rather than a deep bowl, but in this case the stems may need the support of 'Oasis.'

Modern arrangements are best, naturally enough, in modern settings. Often pebbles or water form an integral part of the decoration, and when these are used in a shallow dish a pinholder is essential.

Perhaps this would be the best place to deal with the arranging of large groups of flowers. This seems to daunt many people, but in fact the same principles of technique apply, whether flowers are being arranged in a small vase or in a very large container to form an enormous group. The most important factor to bear in mind is proportion. Few people have much trouble with a display of average size. It is when a much larger composition is planned that they come up against difficulties, which arise mainly from a lack of suitable equipment and material. We cannot stress too strongly the absolute necessity to 'think big.'

The first thing to consider is the pedestal. This must be strong and stable, and although it should not be delicate it must not be cumbersome. Its height is important and without going to extremes the taller the pedestal the better. The container should be large, wide-necked and heavy, to facilitate the arranging and also to add stability. The equipment also demands a certain amount of special attention: the wire netting should be mounded high in the container, to give maximum support to long, unwieldy branches and stems, and the number of tubes and the length of the sticks to which each is attached will depend on the height of the arrangement.

A far more attractive display will be achieved with a limited number of really long, carefully selected stems, and large showy blooms, than with a limitless quantity of short stems and small flowers. We go to immense trouble to obtain foliage long enough to reach from the container to the extremities of a planned arrangement. It would be hard to over-emphasize how much these long branches help the stability and balance of a large group. They give a firm basis on which to build the whole composition. If the background material is so short that it has to be placed in tubes it frequently causes trouble as the arrangement progresses, by swivelling out of position on account of its weight. This can give the arranger some terrible moments of panic. The outline flowers, as well as foliage, should be as long as possible. The fewer the tubes required, the more attractive the end result.

The material used to form the face should be as showy as possible. Because of the need for size and impact at the focal point we frequently use whole pot plants, such as hydrangeas, azaleas or poinsettias, instead of cut flowers. They are prepared in the following manner. Knock the plant out of the pot and gently shake the loose soil from the roots. Then, wrap the root-ball firmly in polythene. Two canes are then struck into the bottom of the root-ball and their other ends are wedged firmly into the wire netting. The angle of the canes in relation to the plant can be adjusted to make the flowers face whichever way is required, and their length altered to give the right height. Three or more pot plants can be supported in this way to form the centre of a large group. You will find that there is in fact very little difference in basic principle between constructing a large group and arranging one of average size.

It is more satisfactory with any arrangement, to do it 'in situ' but if this is not possible try to find a working surface of approximately the same height as the surface on which the flowers will be placed eventually.

In the final stages of an arrangement people are often tempted to overwork their creation, and so spoil its original spontaneity. This springs from the natural desire to use all the material to hand, rather than have any left over. But it is essential to know when to stop. Say to yourself, 'When in doubt, leave it out.'

When any arrangement is finished and in position, do remember to top up the vase with water. It is surprising how easy it is to forget this very basic part of flower arranging.

All the principles mentioned so far, and illustrated throughout the book, are taught in our school. The courses vary in duration from one whole day to six weeks of weekly classes. The wide variety of people attending these courses includes housewives who wish to decorate their homes, and nurses and receptionists who find it useful to be able to do attractive arrangements quickly. Private lessons are very much in demand and are sometimes given in the student's home or hotel. Many people have come to the school for relaxation, or to improve a hobby; some have become so fascinated that they have made flower arranging their career.

If you have a garden you can grow many interesting foliages with which to add shape, colour and texture to your arrangements. But if you have to rely on a florist it is sometimes hard to get variety. In either case you may be glad to supplement what you have available with some of the beautiful things growing abundantly in the countryside. It is most important to remember, however, that wild flowers should never be picked unless they do grow abundantly, and some should never be picked at all. This cannot be stressed too much. It should also be remembered that all hedgerows belong to somebody and are not public property. Few farmers will mind if a limited quantity of common hedgerow material is picked from the roadside, so long as branches are not torn and no other damage is done. If the material required is on farmland, it is only common courtesy to ask permission to pick it. Farmers will seldom object, provided there is no damage to crops or disturbance to domestic and wild life, and no gates are left open. With the hedgerows diminishing, farmers and conservationists are very conscious that the remaining woodlands and hedges are of vital importance, to preserve what is left of our lovely country heritage, and flower arrangers should be extra careful to see that nothing is destroyed.

It is imperative, in the countryside, to use scissors or secateurs for cutting stems. Severe pulling can dislodge the roots of a plant and so destroy it, and trees and bushes also suffer if branches are torn off. When wild flowers are gathered it is important to get them in water as soon as possible, because usually they do not have much substance. It helps to put them in a large polythene bag and then, on arrival home, they can be revived with warm water. Wild flowers have as much beauty as garden flowers, if not more, and should be treated with as much care and attention.

As is demonstrated in many of the illustrations, our love for natural, simple materials is fundamental to our work. We are very thankful that we have so many gardens and estates, all over the country, from which to obtain materials. We owe a great debt of gratitude to our buyer, who goes to enormous trouble to acquire the materials for which we ask, and who also gets up at 3 a.m. to go to the market. Without her efforts the lovely materials would not be available.

Flowers for the Home

In a really dark area the choice of flowers and also of container can make a very great difference. A chest at the foot of the stairs in this country house provided an excellent position for a low 'all-round' arrangement in a basket. The country atmosphere was maintained by the simplicity of style and the choice of informal garden and country materials. Pale pink paeonies, with lovely centres, and wild grasses form a pool of light.

We sometimes wonder why flowers are so important in the home or at any function. The décor may be superb, the pictures beautiful; but without flowers or plants the whole room will be lifeless. Flowers arranged and chosen carefully, then placed in an important position, will give a vibrance of colour and life with a welcoming effect quite different from anything else.

The choice of flowers for a party in your home will be dictated by the type of function – whether it is a cocktail party, dinner party or informal buffet etc. There are several points to remember, which are important at any function. Firstly colour must be carefully considered and flowers should be placed where they will make an impact. Secondly, in our experience it is simplicity, both in the style of arrangement and the selection of material, that makes the flowers attractive and satisfying.

Whatever the setting, the colouring of the décor will determine that of the flowers to a certain extent: modern fabrics often have large designs and sometimes bright colours and flowers placed near them should do nothing more than produce a pool of one of the colours. Not only will they show up well because of their simplicity, but they will give an aura of restfulness. A mixed arrangement, which would be ineffective here, shows to the best advantage against a plain-coloured background, in which case the colour of the flowers could be chosen to pick up the colouring of the upholstery. If the setting is dark it will make an ideal background for an eye-catching arrangement of bright colours.

The available light, natural or artificial, is an important factor and deserves careful thought. Sunlight gives great vividness to the colours, and an arrangement will be much enhanced by it. Some colours do not show up in dim or artificial light and need direct light from a lamp or spotlight, although this should not be too brilliant. Back lighting is to be avoided if possible because the arrangement will lose colour and only the outline and stems will show. Used well, lighting can provide an endless variety of

decorative effects in a room and add to the texture of the flowers and foliage.

The hall is the first place where flowers have an impact on people entering the house. Often it is dark by day and not brightly lit by night, so the colour of the flowers should be important. Often the flowers are seen only in passing. A small arrangement, however enchanting, would be lost. We mostly find that colour is more important than the type of material used and that yellows, orange and shocking pink are most successful.

The choice of colouring for flowers in a drawing-room requires much care, especially for a large display in which colour influence will be strong. The colours of the cushions, rug or a picture may provide some inspiration. It is quite surprising, the extent to which the colouring of flowers may seem to adjust the background colour by emphasizing one element in it. For instance a red arrangement near a picture of a hunting scene will give greater prominence to the huntsmen, whereas blue flowers will give greater prominence to the sky – but do remember that blue flowers tend to disappear in night light.

The character of the house or apartment will have some bearing on the choice of flowers and containers and leave scope for self-expression.

Often it is by a certain amount of trial and error that one decides on the best places for flowers. Sometimes, of course, the opportunities are limited; in a hall for instance, suitable surfaces are usually few, whereas a drawing-room may have many. It is generally preferable to have one important arrangement rather than several smaller ones giving a cluttered effect.

Flowers in the home will give the greatest pleasure if they fit in easily with the surroundings and are not allowed to dominate. Too many flowers in a room can be overwhelming. This of course is purely a matter of judgement; the size of the room and the type of occasion will decide how much decoration may be done to good effect. Where there are to be more than one arrangement, groups will be more effective if placed at different levels, so that their shapes as well as their positions may be contrasting.

A fireplace, as a rule, is not a good place to put flowers, but where it does seem appropriate to do so we have found that simple green arrangements are most decorative. Some foliage plants may be good candidates for this position, but great care must be taken to ensure that they are not subject to draught and lack of light and that the leaves are kept soot-free.

An unusual container, which may have a difficult shape or colour, needs to be filled with very carefully chosen materials. The materials in this arrangement in a pottery tiger's head were chosen for their soft autumn colours, which blend with the colours in the head, and also to make an interesting mixture with plenty of variety of colour, shape and texture. Although the display is heavy it is by no means solid. The outline is formed by delicately-shaped materials, including rose hips, privet berries, trails of passion flower and ivy, which lead into the more solid forms of hydrangea and *Medlar* foliage. The bells and seed heads of *Cobaea scandens* and the gentle texture of a yellow buddleia bring relief to the heaviness of the centre.

In this arrangement in the window of a country house, only garden flowers, mixed with herbaceous flowers and shrubs, were used: paeonies, foxgloves, delphiniums, catmint, 'syringa' and poppies. The size of arrangement requires approximately twelve stems to form the outline, fifteen blooms to give weight to the central part, and twelve stems of intermediate-sized flowers to be placed where most effective.

Right The natural simplicity of this arrangement of mixed white blossom and *Caladium* leaves complements the formality of the Japanese mural painting.

A very informal style of
arrangement in the hall of
Lady Pulbrook's country
house. As the lighting was
not very bright, flowers with
luminous colour and clear
form were chosen. This
arrangement, of yellow
regale lilies, Solomon's seal
(*Polygonatum
multiflorum*), *Hosta
sieboldiana,* lady's mantle
(*Alchemilla mollis*) and
green tobacco (*Nicotiana
affinis* 'Lime Green'),
provides impact and
perfume without being
ostentatious.

A fireplace in summer is
sometimes a difficult area to
decorate, especially when it
is as wide as this one in the
large hall of a Tudor house.
The simple green
arrangement, composed of
four stems of lime tree
flowers, five clumps of wild
iris reeds, ten leaves of
Hosta fortunei 'Alboptica'
and three stems of
Euphorbia wulfenii,
demonstrates how a few
well-chosen stems can make
a large display which is very
decorative but not intrusive.

A lovely arrangement which gives emphasis to an old chest and picks up the lighter beige colours of the painting above, using tulips, alstroemeria, spray chrysanthemum and the sharp green of guelda.

Left A large arrangement on a piano using materials from the garden in late summer: Digitalis, eremurii, garden roses, artichoke leaves, and lilies.

Table Decorations

Requiring very little space
on the table, this is a good
design for a restricted area.
Hyacinth bells, roses,
Helleborus foetidus and
Echeveria were individually
wired, and then the ends of
the wires were twisted
together until there was
sufficient length to form the
garland and the half-circlet.
This type of decoration
should be placed in position
at the last moment.

There is often little space in a dining-room for more than a table decoration, but if there is a mantlepiece this would be ideal for extra flowers. The dining-table is perhaps the most versatile place for flowers.

Harmonizing of colour is fundamental. Although the colouring of the general background should have some bearing on the choice of flowers, for a table decoration this is not really as important as the design of the dinner service and also of the table cloth or mats if these have a coloured pattern. The texture of the tableware should blend in every way. Exotic flowers however lovely would seem quite out of place in conjunction with pottery, but with cut glass, small delicate flowers are needed to show off its beauty. Silver is most accommodating and shows off flowers very well, reflecting their colours and highlights.

Anyone interested in arranging flowers will develop an eye for the container most suitable for a particular type of arrangement. A container is not just a vessel for holding water, but an important part of the total design. A low container is particularly suitable for small dining-tables so that the flowers can be kept well below the eye-level. Many shapes and designs of container are suitable, from a Victorian épergne, which can look breathtaking on a larger table, to individual tiny pots which can give a personal touch. The choice depends on the setting and on the grandeur of the occasion.

Although one central arrangement is the most popular, it is by no means essential. Many of our arrangements have had a central ornament or candelabra with small placement of flowers, or a garland surrounding it. One could also have flower-filled candlecups - these containers are available from florists in silver, gold and black. Candlecups will fit into most candlesticks, whether wood, china or glass, and give an all-round display. Garlanding running down the centre of a wide table looks marvellous if there are important ornaments that need to be displayed.

For more informal settings 'fun' containers can be used – an old china

sauceboat, a copper pot, any type of wooden container, or baskets. Those containers sold by florists usually have a liner, but if you have a container that isn't waterproof either have a liner made or use double polythene which will solve your problem temporarily.

Open-plan living areas are more popular now and bring the kitchen into greater importance. Here, simple flowers such as marigolds, daisies and nasturtiums look right in baskets or containers made of natural materials.

Fruit and vegetables can be used with flowers to give a very lush effect, and we often use a large candle and surround it with a combination of these. If you are having small tables, they can look very attractive with different-coloured flowers and candles on each, such as red, blue, yellow, etc. We have also used fruit in the same way. Indeed, fruit provides a richness and depth of colour, an atmosphere of abundance and harvest and a sense of occasion. One of the advantages of using fruit and vegetables is that since their shapes are more sculptured than those of most flowers, they will often provide an arrangement with both interest and impact. The main danger to avoid, with fruit and vegetables as with anything slightly 'off beat', is that of being gimmicky, and so great care should be taken in choosing a suitable occasion – and also choosing the container and other materials, all of which are factors that greatly affect the style of arrangement. Try to use a fruit in such a manner that if it were to be replaced by a flower the whole essence of the display would be altered, and an integral part in the design would be lacking.

Grapes are perhaps easier to incorporate into arrangements than most other fruits because the branches vary considerably in shape and size. They will appear in keeping with most types of flower, and one branch in a small arrangement or several branches cascading down a pyramid of flowers will add drama.

Highly-glazed French pottery gives brilliant colouring to this London kitchen. Massed marigolds enhance the atmosphere, with their dark centres and dramatic colour and form, and they are also in keeping with the style of décor. The working area of the kitchen is partially concealed by a loosely-arranged display of forsythia. The branches were arranged when the flowers were still in tight bud, so that they could give pleasure for many days as the flowers came into bloom.

In a small dining-room with dark walls the flowers for an intimate 'dinner party' were required to emphasize the delicacy of the glass tableware. So lilies-of-the-valley were chosen, and massed in a goblet containing crumpled wire netting to hold the stems in position. To increase the sense of occasion a secondary arrangement was placed in the mirror-lined alcove.

Right Reflections enhance the romantic atmosphere of this table decoration of mixed camellias. The ends of the stems were wrapped in wet moss to maintain freshness (wet tissue paper would do as well), and the blooms were then laid directly onto the glass table.

Left This dining-room, with sliding doors leading through to the kitchen, combines elegance with a country cottage atmosphere. Decorations for a dinner party were therefore planned to reflect both aspects, as well as to harmonize with the green pottery tableware. The central arrangement has a pottery jar as its base, with an up-ended block of 'Oasis' to support the flowers. It is hard to insert primroses into 'Oasis', and so they were left in bunches. When the ends of the stems were snipped off evenly it was possible to ease the bunches into pre-made holes in the 'Oasis', so covering the 'Oasis' completely. The four small posies on the table extend the colour outwards, and the other posies wired onto the candelabra add to the formality of the occasion. The whole decoration demonstrates the value of using simple flowers imaginatively.

This decoration for an alfresco fork luncheon was composed mainly of fruit and vegetables. Artichokes, mushrooms, runner beans, courgettes, grapes and a few heads of yarrow *(Achillea)* were arranged in a low basket, the style being kept compact to minimize any displacement in the wind.

Flowers for Weddings

Only garden and wild materials were used for the decorations in the small country church at Lambourne End. The two pedestal groups at the chancel steps contained azalea and hawthorn (*Crataegus monogyna*), with the green glow being provided by guelder rose (*Viburnum opulus*), *Euphorbia characias* and Solomon's seal (*Polygonatum multiflorum*). The result, although full of colour, was of great simplicity. The eye is drawn towards the altar by two fountains of white flowers; these were carefully placed so as not to obscure the sculpture on the wall. The ends of the pews were decorated with small posies of cow parsley in small blocks of 'Oasis', with wire hooks to loop over the top of the pews and pieces of polythene placed behind to prevent the 'Oasis' from damaging the wood.

A wedding, above all other occasions, calls for a memorable display of flowers. It is not simply a matter of providing a beautiful setting – we are always very concerned that the bride should have the flowers that will give her most pleasure on her great day. Advance planning is essential, and it is helpful to have discussions both at the church and at the place chosen for the reception.

Often it happens that the bride will have chosen the design and material for her dress and those of bridesmaids – this will have a bearing on the colour of the flowers. All-white always looks marvellous in the church, particularly if it is very dark.

The character of the church, its architecture, and the number of guests to be present are important to bear in mind when planning the arrangements. It is also wise to have a word with the church official, to discover whether they have any definite preference about the positioning of the flowers.

Always bear in mind that there may be other weddings taking place that same day, and the time by which the flowers are to be cleared.

As a rule a large church will need only a few arrangements on a grand scale. The selection of flowers will be influenced by its situation – whether town or country, for example. It is essential to retain the atmosphere of the building. It is polite to ask the church official what decoration is customary in the church, especially in the sanctuary. Flowers on the altar are sometimes not allowed, and pedestal arrangements at the sides have to be the alternative.

Since a large part of the wedding takes place at the chancel steps, it is here that the most impressive groups should be placed. This is the part of the church that is very much under the eye of the guests, and is a good idea to provide as much interest as possible. The entrance looks more welcoming with flowers arranged in a suitable position – perhaps on the font as this is usually near the door. With all these subsidiary arrangements, however, the question of balance should be borne in mind!

A wide centre aisle can be decorated most attractively with small posies attached to the pew ends. Some churches also have balconies and pillars that lend themselves to garlanding and large clusters of flowers.

Synagogues vary in structure and design as widely as churches, and so here too the floral decoration can be varied equally. The Chupa (canopy) however is the most important feature; it is usually most beautiful and of great value. If they are permitted, large clusters of flowers on each corner look handsome with garlanding down the poles. Since these flowers are seen at close quarters, delicate slightly fragrant ones would be most suitable.

A pair of large arrangements are often placed on each side on the ark. If so, large showy blooms are necessary for a better effect. The reading desk is normally near the entrance and in a position that obscures the canopy and so some kind of decoration is needed here. Flowers could be placed on the corners or perhaps on the sconces. Again it depends on the architecture and grandeur of the occasion.

A close-up of the sanctuary showing fountains of flowers in which wild hawthorn predominates. Solidity is provided by Mexican orange (*Choisya ternata*) and rhododendron, and ivy trails cascade over the pedestals. The containers for these arrangements were a pair of four-tiered tins placed in small urns. These tiered tins make it possible for the material to flow downwards in layers, which is so much more attractive than if the stems all come from one point at the top of the pedestals.

The ancient church of St Helen's, Bishopsgate, required decorations that would not obscure the beauty of the building. The large groups at the chancel steps were therefore placed on low pedestals, so that they would not conceal too much of the rood screen. Pink was chosen to blend with the colours worn by the bridesmaids, and also to pick up the pinkish tone in the wood. Heavy wide urns, which gave stability to the groups, were filled with long stems of pink and cream blossom, rhododendron, pots of hydrangea and weeping willow, the colours showing up well against the richness of the background. The altar table was small in proportion to the reredos, and so, to give it importance, two tall pedestal candlesticks decorated with mixed white flowers were placed either side. The flowers included double tulips, hyacinths and trails of stephanotis cascading down the front.

The large clusters of cow parsley were arranged in blocks of 'Oasis', fixed on the balcony and pillars. They continue the theme of the pew ends - a simple but wonderful setting for the entrance of the bride.

Right   A feature has been made of the arch in this tiny country church in Sarratt. The whole theme was white with just a touch of blue in the narrow ribbons used in the posies at the pew ends. The flowers used were lily-of-the-valley, roses, cow parsley and blossom.

Overleaf   At the entrance of the church the font has been decorated with lily-of-the-valley and blue lobelia bringing out the blue of the mosaic behind. Above on the ledge an arrangement of blossom - Solomon's seal and lilies.

46

The Reception

The style for the flowers at a reception will vary considerably according to the kind of place that has been chosen, a hotel, a private house or a marquee.

When a reception is held in an hotel or other public place, the flowers ought to be given great prominence. It is amazing what a difference lovely flowers will make to an impersonal background. The rooms will probably be lofty as well as large and so pedestal arrangements may be the most suitable. An ideal position for a pair of these is the place where the guests are received. The flowers will provide a beautiful frame for the bride and groom, and also a good background for photographs. According to the size of the room or rooms, several other groups may well be needed. These should be kept high so that they can be seen above the heads of the guests. Hanging arrangements are excellent for this purpose and very decorative.

In a private house the normal atmosphere of the home should be preserved as far as possible, which means creating simple, informal displays. Remember the reception rooms are likely to be crowded and it would be sensible to keep the flowers above eye level. A particularly fine arrangement, all the same, will probably be called for in the area where the bride and groom and their parents will receive their guests. This arrangement might be on the mantlepiece or a table. A large display in the hall would give pleasure to the guests as they arrive, and also, perhaps as they stand waiting to be received. Decorations on the staircase would give a wonderful welcome and give an atmosphere of excitement.

A marquee presents a great challenge to the decorator. In the first place, decorating schemes will depend on whether it is framed or one with poles. The latter kind usually has little height at the sides, and so a pedestal arrangement would be ineffective; but the poles, so unattractive in themselves, are splendid for displays since the flowers are kept high and out of the way. As an alternative to this, poles can look most attractive decorated with garlands of flowers twisted around them; this works

The staircase hall of a country house was the setting where a bride was to receive her guests. Garlands of ivy trails were caught up with posies of *Gypsophila elegans* all the way up the bannisters. The pedestal was too tall and heavy for a group to be practicable or attractive, so a low dish with blocks of 'Oasis' was used. The arrangement was designed to have the flowers cascading down, so concealing a great deal of the pedestal. The flowers included 'Virgo' roses, regale lilies, bridal wreath *(Spirea × arguta)* and *Campanula persicifolia,* with *Clematis montana* accentuating the downward flow.

especially well in a small marquee.

Sometimes trellis-work can be incorporated into a marquee. At the entrance, for example, an archway of trellis decorated with flowers looks enchanting. In a framed marquee, the sides can have panels of trellis, which provide an excellent basis for decoration. Although trellis-work is more frequently used in marquees, it can also be used to alter the whole appearance of a room. Once we used panels of trellis in a small room that was to be used as the reception area, and decorated them with branches of camellia in the form of espalier trees. The bride and groom then received their guests in a grotto of flowers.

Whenever a reception is held, the cutting of the wedding cake and speeches will cause all attention to be focused in one direction. We therefore recommend making a feature of the cake, if possible, by giving it a table of its own, and if possible placed on a low dais. A floor length tablecloth of gathered organdie, and a decoration of trailing ivy and smilax or jasmine, with perhaps small posies of flowers at intervals, will create a most romantic setting, set off with two arrangements of flowers. A very long buffet table at a reception can look bleak if no flowers are placed on it. Tall fountains or pyramids of flowers would be ideal here, the height offsetting the length of the table. Care should be taken however to keep these arrangements compact, so that they do not irritate the caterers.

There will be other suitable places for flowers, such as small tables where guests will relax, or a short stairway or passage; these can be kept simple. They may only be seen in passing but what a difference they can make to a memorable day!

The poles of a marquee are always eye-sores, and since the ways of decorating them are very few they present a difficult problem. In this marquee four blocks of soaked 'Oasis' were covered with wire netting and nailed high up on both of the poles, to make a base for the decorations. As daisies were to be featured in all the decorations, the small marguerite (*Chrysanthemum frutescens*) was the main type of flower; it is similar in size to the wild dog daisy. The marguerites were left on their root ball and arranged as whole plants. Sprays of *Philadelphus* gave additional length and white roses provided 'punch'.

Far right The buffet table in the marquee was decorated with flowers arranged in tiered tins set in bronze urns. The urns gave the arrangements great stability, which is essential when flowers are to be placed where they could easily be knocked over. Daises, 'Iceberg' roses and *Helleborus foetidus* were used here, continuing the theme for all the decorations at the reception.

52

An archway of trellis at the entrance to a marquee was simply decorated with ivy trails and single white spray chrysanthemums. Small blocks of 'Oasis' were fixed onto the trellis at varying intervals, to keep the flowers fresh throughout the reception. This type of decoration is possible throughout the year, except for the short season in early summer when the new growth of ivy can be very soft.

Right The cake table for a reception at Trinity House illustrates the advantage of making a feature of the wedding cake. The table also draws attention to the fine window which gave the bride a beautiful backcloth as she cut the cake. The white organdie cloth was decorated with garlands of ivy trails caught up with clusters of gardenias, and on the top tier of the cake was a small posy of lilies of the valley. Two fountains of white flowers flanked the table to give it additional importance. In these the flowers used were white cherry blossom, 'Actaea' narcissus, double white tulips and hydrangeas, with the lovely white and green marbled leaves of *Caladium* to give fullness and variation of texture.

THE TRINITY HOUSE OF
DEPTFORD STROND 1514

DEPTFORD. RATCLIFF AND
STEPNEY IN THE 16ᵗʰ AND
17ᵗʰ CENTURIES.

WATER LANE LONDON 1660
DESTROYED IN THE
GREAT FIRE 1666 AND
REBUILT. DESTROYED BY
FIRE IN 1715 & REBUILT
TOWER HILL LONDON 1795

PARTIALLY DESTROYED
BY ENEMY   1940
REBUILT

Party Flowers

This large group, extending the whole length of the mantlepiece and half-framing the mirror, is set in a long low tin and contains mixed May-time flowers with a few 'all the year round' chrysanthemums. Although this was arranged for a wedding it would be a suitable decoration for any important function.

There is no substitute for flowers to set the right atmosphere, whatever the occasion. We always enjoy doing flowers for parties, but it is most disappointing when time is too short for us to gather in all the materials we would like to use. Many of the flowers and foliage that we particularly value come from private gardens, and it takes time to do all the ordering and collecting. So we appreciate being given as much notice as possible. Even with flowers from the market, we need time. Different flowers may take varying times to reach their best condition, and all of them should have a good drink before being arranged. If you are going to do the flowers yourself, take care to allow plenty of time.

Cocktail parties, receptions and any large gathering of people require that some of the flowers should be above shoulder level so that they can be seen. A mantlepiece would be ideal for carrying a large display, or a tall-boy or pedestal. Again the focal points are important – it is always welcoming and flattering to have flowers where you are being received. Mirrors can also be used to effect, and double the amount of flowers with reflection.

A doorway looks more important with a group either side which could consist of columns or fountains of flowers, or even be garlanded. A buffet table or bar looks lovely with a pyramid of fruit and flowers. Space is always at a premium and waiters prefer something which is more compact and not in their way.

In a large ballroom set for a dinner dance the tables are important and it is the quality of imagination that makes it a talking point. The choice depends on the grandeur of the party. Although one central arrangement is the most popular it is by no means essential.

For a large reception or 'coming out' dance, flowers need to be arranged in big striking displays that will match the proportions of the room. It is here that pedestals come into their own – remember that one or two really large groups are more effective than several smaller ones. Generally speaking these are best left to the professional for they are so much more demanding

than you might think, requiring a wide range of knowledge born of experience, and a lot of time and planning. Plaques of fruit and flowers on a wall look lovely and leave the floor area clear when space is at a premium. For a dreary hall we made large frames of moss and hessian and then created pictures of fruit and flowers, rather like Dutch Old Masters, and then lit them accordingly.

Sometimes we are given a theme for a party – this is always fun and creates great atmosphere. We have included one photograph of a tropical scene and although it shows only a section it will give some idea of how birds and animals can be used.

Trees of many shapes and forms can be created with bare branches and foliage, flowers or ferns. We have also used bare trees with fruit and then with special lighting created a very shadowy and mystical atmosphere. For a carnival or hallowe'en party masks made from nuts, seed heads, flowers or fruits are very amusing and unusual. Box hedging made into an archway can create a new entrance, and hedging can cover an ugly bandstand and make it look as though it is part of the garden. For a party in the city we created pendant garlands in the Grinling Gibbons manner to frame magnificent gold plate.

Massed hydrangeas on a buffet table make a striking impression in a large room where a delicate arrangement would have been lost. This is an example of how an arrangement of only one type of flower can have great effect.

Fruit and vegetables are used prominently in these buffet table pyramids for a punch party given at the Waldorf Hotel. The weight of the bronze urns meant that the arrangements could be safely built up with heavy materials. Berries and variegated foliages give a flowing effect, and gold garnette roses were the only flowers used.

Right   One of a pair of massive pyramids composed of garden roses which were the sole decoration for a large reception in Westminster Hall, London. The outline is softened with sprays of rose hips and old man's beard, and fullness is given by croton plants and hydrangeas. The simplicity of the material heightened the dramatic quality of the decorations in this magnificent setting.

Left   A large group of mixed berries, autumn foliages and flowers at the Waldorf Hotel. The position was a difficult one, partly because of the varied background and partly because the group was to stand against a pillar and so would be visible from several angles. The materials were chosen to make a mixture of great variety. They included *Pyracantha, Cotoneaster, Stephanandra,* crab apple and old man's beard, with the lovely form of *Mahonia japonica,* the maroon heads of *Sedum spectabile,* and hydrangeas to make up the centre, and the varying shapes of love-lies-bleeding (*Amaranthus caudatus* 'Viridis'), pineapple flower (*Eucomis*) and Golden Clarion lilies to give additional interest and movement.

The theme of the party was a Caribbean island, and as the place was a large London ballroom there was a great area to transform. In the background are tall branches of evergreen oak (*Quercus ilex*), hung with oranges or lemons, and rhododendrons and azaleas to provide suitable colouring. In the foreground were tropical green plants, bougainvilleas and hibiscus, with coconuts, coolie hats, fish baskets and nets for 'local colour' and parrots for a touch of fun. This type of decoration demands much improvisation if the effect is to be achieved as economically as possible.

Flowers for Christenings

A little font in a country church was decorated with a collar of small blue and white flowers. These were set in 'Oasis', which was secured in position by 'Oasis' tape, and they included lilies-of-the-valley, bluebells, cow parsley and spurge.

All special occasions in our lives are occasions for flowers. For a christening, even though we probably assume that the most important person there is too small to appreciate the surroundings, the occasion can be greatly enhanced by flowers if they are arranged with care and imagination.

The font is naturally where one would want to place flowers, but the extent to which it is decorated may well depend on the preference of the officiating clergy. One of the prettiest arrangements, if permitted, is a circlet of flowers around the rim of the font, and perhaps flowing softly down the sides. At the place where the minister or priest will be standing the circlet should obviously be kept low, to prevent it becoming an impediment during the service.

The flowers used should be small and delicate and unsophisticated as possible. Sometimes it will be possible to follow tradition and have blue flowers for a boy, or pink for a girl, but when two or three babies are to be baptized at the same ceremony, white or pale yellow might be more suitable. We find that pale colours, with their light-giving qualities, always show up best. Furthermore, they give an air of simplicity which is often more appropriate, particularly in country churches.

If for any reason it is not possible to place flowers on the rim of the font, an arrangement at the base can be very decorative. This of course, would only be suitable if the base was built up, so that the flowers were not on the floor and in danger of being trodden on. One delightful decoration we did at the base of the font was made up of moss and bark with clusters of primroses. It gave an impression of woodland simplicity and had a fresh charm that could not have been achieved with more sophisticated flowers. Sometimes families have their own silver bowls which they like to use and again these may be decorated in different ways.

A beautiful stone font
decorated with winter
jasmine, single spray
chrysanthemums, freesia,
roses and variegated trails of
ivy, with just a touch of pale
blue from the hydrangeas.

Flowers for Giving

This pyramid, suitable for a small buffet or side table, is composed mainly of camellias, jasmine (*Jasminum polyanthum*) and guelder roses (*Viburnum opulus*). The lacey quality of the jasmine combines well with the chased silver vase. The base of the decoration is three blocks of 'Oasis' firmly fixed together with a cane and wrapped round with wire netting. With this kind of base there was no difficulty in placing the short-stemmed camellias.

Hospitals are busy, bustling places that are clinical and rather austere, and any type of flowers or flowering plants give the greatest pleasure not only to the patients but to the staff.

There are of course certain practical points that should be remembered. Firstly, there is usually very little space, and secondly, the staff are so busy that they have very little time to arrange flowers no matter how much they enjoy doing so. You may also like to consider the temperature of the room as to the type of flowers you will choose. Heavily perfumed flowers are not always appreciated when someone is very ill, but enjoyed more during convalescence.

From experience we have found the initial sight and impact of the flowers most important. An arrangement of flowers or a tied bunch of flowers, ready just to place in a container are an instant success. Plants in pretty containers are also cheerful and last too. A child may be more amused by receiving flowers in an original container such as a bird, animal or car. Bowls of bulbs such as hyacinths are interesting for the patient, as they can watch them grow; amaryllis are also ideal as they take up very little space, but the impact of the first bloom is breathtaking.

A beautiful container can double as a gift to keep, but it is wiser to choose these when the patient has returned home. It is not always easy to carry all the pots and containers home from hospital and therefore we usually choose something inexpensive and put the value into the flowers.

People often forget how important it is to receive something lovely on returning home after a serious illness; this is a moment that can be very lonely and to receive a lovely gift of flowers no matter how small can bring great joy.

To make this small 'tree' a small block of wet 'Oasis' was firmly fixed to the end of a stick. The other end of the stick was wedged into the pot with moss, and then the 'Oasis' was covered with a selection of spring flowers and foliages to form a loosely-shaped ball. The materials include *Echeveria*, guelder rose, hyacinth, ivy and periwinkle. A few springs of rosemary were placed in the moss to off-set a top-heavy appearance.

Far left A posy of mixed garden flowers which would give interest and pleasure for a long time. All the material was conditioned and given a long drink before being 'arranged' in the hand and tied up with bast. On arrival all that was necessary was to cut the ends of the stems and place the tied bunch in a vase. The jug shown here was very suitable because it could not easily be knocked over.

A low bowl makes an excellent container for a gift of flowers already arranged. Besides being easy to transport, the arrangement will be a practical size on a crowded hospital locker. The flowers include Christmas roses *(Helleborus niger)*, grape hyacinths *(Muscari)* and primroses. These are set among pieces of bark, and sprigs of flowering currant *(Ribes)* and trails of ivy soften the outline.

For the first child born into a family the fantasy and excitement of receiving a stork filled with flowers is wonderful. The stork itself can be re-used and looks magnificent in the nursery for years to come.

Left It is a lovely idea to give something special for the birth of newly born baby; this is a cane cradle filled with flowers, hyacinth pips and freesia and finished with tulle, lace and ribbons. The china swan next to it has been filled with small spring flowers.

Christmas Decorations

A combination of antique and modern is illustrated by this candlestick arrangement of holly and lichen-covered branches in the modern decor of a restaurant.

At Christmas many of us still long to see the age-old traditional decorations repeated, although we now do many variations on the theme. The basic traditional materials still remain the same – holly, mistletoe, ivy and of course the Christmas tree.

Various practical matters, however, must be considered. How long for example must the decorations last? If it is to be placed in a shop window, as part of a display of gifts, it will be arranged many weeks before Christmas and so it must be durable. The widespread use of artificial materials arises naturally from this fact also because we live in centrally heated houses where the dry atmosphere reduces the life span of fresh material. Artificial materials skilfully made up look very effective, and then can be packed away for another year.

Seasonal colours – the red of the holly berries, white of the mistletoe and greens of ivy and conifer – may need to be emphasized in a Christmas decoration by additional flowers and fruits. Red, perhaps the most difficult colour to augment, will be found in scarlet carnations and also roses, and of course the poinsettias. White is easier to supplement; arum and longiflorum lilies, chrysanthemums, poinsettias and forced lilac are all easily obtainable plus many other smaller flowers. It is especially attractive to have fresh arrangements and large groups give great impact. Smaller arrangements could be suitable for a friend in hospital, and your table arrangement could look attractive with candles added.

Candles do add tremendously to any festive occasion and can be incorporated into many different styles. But a note of caution – there is the obvious danger of a decoration being knocked over, especially if young children are going to be running about, and there is also the danger of the flame burning low and catching the foliage. Holly becomes dry and brittle, as do larch and cones; they are all highly inflammable.

How a tree should be decorated is a matter of personal choice. Invariably, however, the simpler the decoration the more effective it is. It might consist

Red peppers and scarlet carnations give brilliance and impact to this pyramid for a buffet table. Fruit-bearing branches of *Malus sargentii* take the colour throughout the arrangement, and cones give solidity to the centre. The variegated holly is contrasted in both colour and texture with *Senecio maritima* and blue rue (*Ruta graveolens* 'Jackman's Blue').

of only one or two colours and a strictly limited variety of ornaments. Although baubles and tinsel are attractive they are by no means essential. For example a tree decorated with glittered cobwebs, cones, and glass icicles with a string of fairy lights all of one colour can be breathtaking. One of the most successful alternatives to a traditional tree is a 'tree' made out of bare branches. For some people this may be the better choice, because of space or because of the setting. Again this can be decorated in a similar way.

Door rings are increasingly popular and are usually made from holly or a combination of holly, pine and cones and finished with a large red ribbon.

Kissing rings, rightly, are a most popular decoration, and are also made from winter foliages and berries, finished with a red bow on top and bottom with a sprig of mistletoe tucked into the bottom. It is traditional to have small apples inside the ring but baubles are also pretty. Another delightful hanging decoration is the mistletoe ball, finished with either a red or a white ribbon.

Children look forward to Christmas with mounting excitement and the actual day can seem a long time away to them. The gap can be filled by an advent ring; this is a simple ring made of evergreens into which five candles are set. The first candle is lit on Advent Sunday, the others on each successive Sunday and the fifth on Christmas Eve.

Swagging is very effective and can be made in any length, for fire-places, stairs, doorways and columns; it looks lovely when the colouring tones with the room. There are many different ideas, all original, that can be created that will transform the whole of the atmosphere of Christmas.

It is a delight too, at Christmas to have a reminder that spring is not too far away. What a joy it is to see the first Christmas rose, and the scented hyacinth and paper-white narcissus which will perfume a whole room, and particularly for the New Year before once again all the seasons revolve before us.

This traditional kissing ring is formed from three hoops and decorated with cones and sprigs of holly and *Cupressus*. Apples were strung in the centre and underneath, and the red was emphasized by ribbon bows at the top of the hoops and also below, where a bunch of mistletoe was fixed.

Right Red poinsettias have been used through the centre of this group with wonderful foliages including variegated holly, leucothia, cotoneaster, eucalyptus and larch, which have been lightened with hydrangea heads and a little senecio; the red euphorbia links the red of the poinsettias and berries.

A marble fireplace which has been decorated with artificial swagging, giving a very festive air. We have used artificial pine, mistletoe and waxy golden fruits.

Candles predominate in this table arrangement, using fresh fruits, blue pine,
larch and variegated ivy.

Swagging used on a very pretty pine staircase caught up with bronze silk bows,
again using artificial pine, fruits and nuts.

A traditional Christmas tree
decorated simply with gold
baubles, gold lights and
bronze silk bows.
This theme is carried
through to the pyramid of
artificial fruits and nuts on
the small table.

Flowers for Children

A teddy bear is made with wire netting and moss in the same way as a squirrel, but slightly more easily since the frame is stockier and has a less demanding shape. The head and body are covered with small double chrysanthemums, which have been taken off at the head and pinned on with wires bent like hair pins. Lichen moss is used for the paws and the inside of the ears, and ivy berries for the eyes and nose. A big bow is tied around the neck to give an attractive finish. The teddy bear should be stable enough to sit upright, whereas the squirrel sometimes requires the support of a larger base to keep it steady.

No one who has seen the expression of wonder and delight in the eyes of a child clutching a bunch of flowers can doubt the reality of that unconscious joy. It is a joy that endures, we find, even though we are surrounded by flowers all day long, and have had to deal with the many difficulties that they can present.

To encourage young children in their instinctive appreciation of both wild and garden plants is to give them an interest which may grow with the years, and play a valuable part for the rest of their lives. There are a great many ways to foster this interest. Nearly all children love an 'adventure' walk in the country; their interest is kept alive by the discovery of leaves and small flowers. It is on walks such as these that a child will enjoy collecting the wild flowers that grow in such profusion and learn to recongnize and appreciate them.

A birthday, to a child, is all-important, and memories of early birthdays will survive a lifetime. One way of celebrating at the beginning of the day is to lay a crescent or circlet of flowers around the child's plate on the breakfast table. It need take only a short time to do and can be made from pretty 'bits' from the garden.

A party is something every child looks forward to for days before the event, and although food is undoubtedly important, flowers specially chosen will not go unnoticed. A tiny posy on each plate gives each child something to take home, and no party is complete without that. A garland around the birthday cake singles this out for special attention. Of all the things we do for children's parties, perhaps the most memorable are the cuddly teddy bears and other animals.

This squirrel, made from a wire netting shape filled with moss, with lichen moss pinned on to form the coat, is an example of how attractive an animal can be. It will remain fresh for a long time if it is placed in the garden in a sheltered position. Larch cones decorate the pieces of bark which form the base and give the squirrel extra stability.

Overleaf   This enchanting photograph and the one which follows demonstrate the variety and skill of our workroom staff. They show two scenes from the Beatrix Potter stories - this one is the winter scene with Jemima Puddle Duck. The base of the birds is made from moss, then the feathers have been made from tulip petals and all the clothing 'made to measure'.

This spring scene shows Benjamin Bunny standing in a woodland filled with flowers, primroses, snowdrops, rhododendrons, maidenhair ferns, and variegated hosta leaves. The animals this time have been covered with reindeer moss.